CW01270468

Heart Strings

Forever Wanderer

Holly Coop

Heart Strings

Forever Wanderer

Copyright © 2017 Holly Coop

IISBN: 10-979-8-9911032-1-3
ISBN: 13-979-8-9911032-1-3

Cover Photo by Emma Coop
Cover Design by Mauverneen Blevins

Other titles by this author

A Cup of Inspiration to Go Please –
My Heart Runneth Over

Locks of Love – A Book of Encouragement

A Line in the Sand –
A Journey Towards Forgiveness

Contents

Contents

Contents

Here's to moonlit nights
And those we share them with

Hold my cape, dear
There is a party right next door -
It will change our lives - forevermore.

My forever wanderer
If the cape fits – wear it

Love at First

Eyes meet
Uniting souls

A cosmic reaction
Where love unfolds

The cards of their lives
Will they play or fold?

Only time will tell
What the universe already knows

Soul mate + Passion ≈ Fate?

Come, breathe with me
Through all eternity

Soul mate
Two hearts – two bodies
Together forming one

Passion
A combustible reaction
Hearts engulfed in passion

Fate
Does the universe align its stars just so?
That neither party can know?
What turns their lives are about to take
When they leave it all up to fate?

When love aims its arrow
No heart is safe

Does the universe align its stars just so?
Soul mate + passion ≈ fate

Fire Starter

I know I am playing with fire
But the warmth keeps drawing me in
What harm is there in wishful thinking
If I do not
Sin?

The elements are against me
I cannot win
When love's flame ignites a lonely heart
To the passion that stirs within

I know I am playing with fire
But the warmth keeps drawing me in
How can a lonely heart defend
From a burning desire so intense?

My logic whispers
Stay away
While my heart screams
Jump right in

Desire My Heart

A woman's heart's desire
Undeniably unleashed through her flesh
Surely -
It would be a mistake
To deny her thirst, to be quenched

A fool may underestimate
The struggle she must bear to maintain
When a woman - is forced to tame
The smoldering heat - kindled
Underneath her passion's flame

A woman's heart's desire
Unbridled against his flesh
Surely -
It would be a mistake
To deny her thirst, to be quenched

Divided Heart

A divided heart once whole
No longer beating as one
Once joy-filled
Now empty – void of love

Divided – broken in two
A red heart-colored blue
A heart rendered, powerless
By forbidden love, shown
Cast used
to beat alone

Time passes slowly
For a heart wading in lonely
Into the sea, it's severed – free
Riding the wave of sorrow
Drifting spirits carried along
Mirrored images of her own
Caught in a current of sad
Unable to rise above
Struggling to stay afloat
While heartstrings tugged

Searching now for rescue – a buoy – a rope
A brightly burning beacon of the promise, of Hope
Perhaps another mate whose heart, drenched in holes
Where mine can share with theirs
And theirs can call mine – home

Fickle Hearts

Oh lord, our hearts, they are so fickle
They know not what they want
Or is it just our deceiving minds
Tapping upon their open door?
Filling them with the uncertainty
Of our fleeting thoughts
Misguiding them in what they inherently know?
Oh lord, on which path should this fickle heart go?

Same Time Next Year

In love and whole again

A heart once chipped to pieces,
Your love has been the glue

What would I have become
Had I not found a friend in you?

Your kindness took away the grief
That once paralyzed me from life

One kiss from you breathed fresh air into
The suffocating sadness that engulfed me every night

Your touch melted away the hardness
that once shielded the woman in me
Penetrating the barrier encrypting a soul
That longed to be set free

Once residing in heartache and pain,
Forgetting that love can be true,
My faith restored
By the love I have found with you

You made me believe in me
Your passion renewed a spirit
Once laden with hardship and grief
Tapping into my memory to recall
That life at its boiling point
Leaves a taste of bittersweet
But to all who remain alive in it
It's a glorious gift indeed

Halting my heartache with unbridled love
The pain I suffered - brought to an end

What would my world have become
 had I not found you in it, my friend?

A heart once chipped to pieces
In love and whole again

Call Me

I wait with desperate longing -
For my phone to ring once more
I attempt to within the confines of my mind
To stir his to call
Oh, how I desire to hear his voice
Whisper sweet nothings into my ear
And softly kiss my neck
As he draws my body near
Precious fleeting moments
My heart will forever hold dear

Silently, I wait and wonder
If I will ever again hear his voice
Anticipation of what is only my heart's dream
Is making it hard for this body to function
In life's reality

And although my head knows the truth
That love's blind eyes refuse to see
My heart continues to in silence scream

Call me

Questions

I miss you terribly
I am feeling very jumbled up today
Emotionally
Many feelings
Many questions
Flooding my brain
I'm dying to call and talk to you
Not knowing what to say
Why does the condition of one's heart
Complicate the head this way?

To think with your heart
And feel with your head
For me, it hasn't worked thus far
Is it because if a soul
Is not in the place where it should be
Will force a heart to wander
In search of its destiny?

Is there a soul mate
That each was born to find?
How will I know if you are mine?

Questions
So many questions
When it's answers that I need
Perhaps my foolish heart will wander
For eternity
Until it unites with the soul mate
For which it seeks

Picking Up Pieces

I fear that you will break my heart
And there are not enough pieces left
To break apart
My head is screaming run away
My heart is leaping directly in the way
Of the pierce, from your love's aim

In the Palm of

I feel as though I hold a lot of hearts in my hand
And that I am deserving, of none
I pray I make the right choice of whom
I hand over my own to
Who will be the one?

Advice Worth Taking

Two little birdies whispered in my ear
Words I needed to hear

"I don't think that we can choose who we love
But only how we love them", spoken by d.

"I don't think we can control
our hearts", spoken by e.

"Thank you", heard by h.

Love's Affair

We crave each other
To the point that neither one can sleep
Neither one can eat

Do we dare?
Until love's arrow penetrates barriers buried deep
Breaking down all the boundaries existing between
Two hearts might never embrace a unified beat
To satiate a passion felt extreme

Unfair!
Harboring desire intense beyond belief
Two bodies destined to be one - for all eternity
Where neither will need food - neither will need sleep
And time will only exist – far beyond their reach

Vulnerabilities bared
Longing to lie in each other's arms
Protected by love's cocoon
Two hearts in love over the moon

Will anyone care?
Hidden from judgment and silent stares
In a secret little private place
On the outskirts of anywhere
Where time too slowly will pass by

On the days I cannot see him, I feel so out of sorts
And on the days I do, my mood seems to float
How much longer must I wait until he is mine?
As time too slowly passes by
On a love affair collision course, they ride

Breathe

Soul mate
Passion mate
Come ~ breathe with me
Through all eternity

Jealousy

Blue eyes can turn a green hue
No claims
No restrictions
Neither of them holds
Leave their lives empty, their hearts feeling cold
No commitments nor promises was the rule they set in stone
Now, neither can keep, as feelings do unfold

So goes the story of two hearts
Heading down a path
When not straight or narrow, neither stands a chance
escaping cupid's arrow, where green-eyed monsters clash

He thinks it's cute
when all her sentences seem to rhyme
And when hand in hand, they walk
Their feet keep in perfect time
She adores the way his excitement bubbles
When she walks into the room
And the way he notices the sparkle in her green eyes
When they become immersed in his clear, water-blue

She enjoys his wit
He melts in her charm
Together to embrace life arm in arm

No holds barred, just a mention from the past
Hook, line, and sinker, both sunk fast
Neither can deny the love they feel inside
Bringing all past rules to a halt

Simply
When hearts begin to care, neither wants to share
I guess it was just par for the course
when love sets its sights on the pair
All their romance preconditions fell apart

Moving On

Glad you found another
To take my place
Fill in your blanks
Just another pretty face?
Perhaps -
Some things are best
Left to fate
Hearts are safer that way

Winners' vs Losers

How can you bring back feelings,
Once replaced?
How does one agree to stay
When a new start they crave?
How do you force your heart to choose
What society says is "the right" thing to do?
What is a new beginning for some
Is an end for another one.
A heart once happy, now sad
A heart once sad, now glad

There is no right or wrong answer, or so I'm told
When you are dealing with complications of the soul
Whichever the outcome, feelings are hurt
No matter how delicate we tread on shaky ground
The ego will bruise
When someone lost, another found
Two will wind up winners
With at least one heart destined to lose.

How sweet can victory be?
When won at the expense of another
Leaves, a bitter taste indeed
Two hearts entangled, wrapped helplessly around
In the existence of one soul, a heart is forever bound

Which one will be lost?
Which one found?
Which one will she keep?
Sometimes fate leaves our hearts,
With a taste of bittersweet.
Winner vs loser – which one will she be?

Universal Energies

I feel like the universe is whirling around me
In tune with every emotion, I am feeling
All its elements attempt to shed light
On answers that I seek
To questions that are mounting over me

People from my past have come back into view
Showing me that the love still shines
And even during years when visits cease
Thoughts are never few
Our lives remain entwined

Old flames ignited, still show signs of spark
Eliminating an old, harbored doubt
Clarifying that hearts that once were captured
Are not easily let loose
Everything and all are simply the universe
Keeping its close watch over you

Taking Attendance

I have heard it said that absence often results
in hearts growing fonder
While too much may cause love to wane
In the past, it has been my experience
The ladder is what usually came

Take caution in how much time you let tick away
What a tragedy when we allow our loves to fade
Balance can be tricky when you are dealing with love
Every moment is a gamble when hearts are at stake

If you are lucky, it can last forever
If you are foolish, it might slip away
Absence can cause a heart to grow fonder or drift away
What a tragedy - when love begins to fade
Be present with your love -- today

Face It!

You are not as connected to his heartstrings
As your heart likes to think
Be calm
Move on
Accepting that love stinks!

Free

Technically speaking, you may be free,
But that certainly is not true of your emotions
Which are all in a tangle
Since your heart has been "captured" by me
If you are feeling that you are in a snare
Unwilling to admit how much you care
Perhaps I should loosen my grip
Walk away and quit

Roller Coaster

Is it possible for the dizzying of a "roller coaster" to finally
cause one to see clearly?
Emotional ups
Emotional downs
A spinning heart gets tossed around
Decision made
Clarity once again fades

Relying on feelings not only of your own
You attempt to decipher truth from words alone
Though contradicted by actions shown
Leaving a soul with questions
Its future suspended mid-air
When a heart falls in love
How is the soul to fare?

A task left to one alone
To fill in blanks with answers unknown
Hearts dangle aimlessly on worn-out sleeves
Broken, they are left to bleed

Unable to share in their grief
Emotions in motion and gathering speed
The dizzier the mind becomes
Clearer the vision to see
Into the heart that bleeds

Emotional ups
Emotional downs
A spinning heart gets tossed around
Without the courage to finally let go
The wandering soul might never know
What its lonely heart needs
 and how to set it free

Once Upon a Time

True love or fairy tale?
What's the difference?
Once so in love
Now so done
Once so unsteady
Now so ready
To live
With or without your love

Two Broken Hearts

I
Have been hurt
You
have been hurt
This for sure
We know
Maybe with
Our broken pieces
We
Can form a whole

What's Love Got to Do with It?

I have had enough of this love stuff
I am ready now to have some life

You

I love the way you know me
How you see right through my walls
When the song my heart is singing
There's no reason to its rhyme
For some, that would be enough
To give up and say goodbye

But you are not that kind of a guy
You care enough to stay close by
Dig down deep for those reasons why
Unafraid of pulling up from the surface
Feelings that refuse to subside
Where hurt comfortably reside

And when my only desire
Is to hide and lose myself from life
You are there to illuminate
My surrounding darkness with your light

Through my stained-glass-walls
You can see
Exactly, what is troubling me

Without a single word spoke
You know what I am feeling
With your strength, I find myself able to cope

Although it has taken many years and made mistakes
I knew the very day we met we were each other's fate
Like two puzzle pieces, we seemed to connect
Never will my heart hold regret

The fire in your eyes ignites in me a spark
Enlightened, now I see
All that had once been blind in my dark
If ever we are forced by chance or by choice
To utter the word goodbye
You will be the most cherished memory
My heart will forever hold inside

Roaming Eyes in Disguise

Wow, slap me in the face and open my eyes
Some prefer the chase,
Better than the capture
It's the same old story – chapter after chapter
Now, who can blame – when boredom follows same
The wanderer, from what his passion craves
When the sight of someone new
Ignites
His inextinguishable flame?

With tempting choices – why stop at one?
A single serving would merely be a sampler
And keeping many aids with his avoiding capture

His familiar prowl becomes the norm
To the wounded, he scorned
Their lonely hearts devoured
Once the love begins to fade
But to the one whose eye wanders
To see his cowardice, he fails

Roaming eyes, keep looking
See if you can catch this one that's booking
While you prefer the chase more than the capture
The story ends here, for me
For you, it just begins another chapter

Aftershocks

My heart
Broken into pieces
Stomped on and left forever scarred and stained
Yet still beating
Love, and kindness remain flowing through my veins

What future will be for the broken-hearted?
When they have ransomed, theirs away to a thief?
What hope is there for this heart
Tortured and laden with grief?
Solitude engulfs the daylight
Shadows of gloom dominate the night
In between only lies twilight, where she lingers in her plight

Tormented memories persistently echo
In an already unsettled mind
She wanders around aimlessly
Emotionally deaf, dumb, and blind
A grave of loneliness surrounds her existence
Leaving bitterness to dictate her fate
Finally, by force of habit
Sheer will wrestle her senses awake

Rising with head held high
She moves forward toward the open door
She wonders what will greet her from the unknown side

Forbidden tears flowing
She resists the urge to cry
Turning her cheek once again
She bids the past goodbye
The aftershocks
No doubt
Will be hard
The shake-up may well last long
But just as she has done before
Standing strong
She will carry on

My heart
Broken into pieces
Stomped on and left forever scarred and stained
Yet still beating,
Love, and kindness remain flowing through my veins

Busy Bee

Can't you see
You are building walls
Around loving me
Such busyness
An excuse, my guess
To keep love from getting too close
Perhaps the busy bee's desire
Is to keep his heart unknown

To be forever free
That is the life of the busy bee
It does not leave much choice - for the broken-hearted
Except to pick up the pieces and flee

In My Own Little Corner –
In My Own Little World

Girl once loved boy
Boy once loved girl
Somewhere in the corner of my mind, you are there
No matter how hard I try to forget
I feel the passion of your stare
My concentration lacks
My mind keeps fluttering back
To a moment I will forever hold in my heart
How will this body that aches for yours
Survive love's absence
With your depart

I imagine your touch caressing my outline in the dark
Then, my memory awakens me to the reality that
Our lives have drifted apart
Blood still flows through veins
From a heart whose beat has stopped
Only the taste of your lips against mine
Could cause it to restart

Somewhere in the corner of my mind
There is a secret place for memories to reside
Memories, bittersweet of a passion we once knew
Somewhere in the corner of my mind
I see only you

Tangled Webs

Oh, what tangled

One had an affair that destroyed a marriage
Now, another must have one to save it

When first we practice deceit

It Takes Love to Know Love

With tender feelings shared
Love's beat quickens
Passion ignites with a glow
But
Emotions held in silence – a heart's secret never told
Just as rapidly – love can slow
Beating hearts in love – need to be told
To know

Little Voice

Hello there, little voice
It's been a long time
Since I have allowed you to speak
I have kept you muffled in my head
So, I could continue doing as I please
My heart now aches from the actions
That kept me from hearing you
Now I am at a loss for words
And I don't know what to do

I allowed my heart to get stolen
By a thief that lies in the night
He keeps his heart sheltered
While holding mine tight
Sharing only on his terms
He keeps his emotions safe at bay
He has mastered his art of juggling
With many hearts - his game of play
And though my mind shouts, run along
With him, my heart remains

My head repeats as the world sees
Assuring this is wrong of me
Yet when we are together
My mood dances upbeat
My lips tingle with a happy song
Every time ours meet
My whole life is the only ransom
He says he will accept
The question then remains
Will the payout breed regret?

All his talk of others
Leads me to wonder where we are at
If only he would show me
Without holding back
And stop filling up our time
With all the tit for tat
There is no easy answer
I wish he would let me know
Is my love secure in his?
Or am I just another heart
He will let go

Hanging Moon

The moon is hanging low tonight -
The stars are flickering up above
And I will be here until morning's light
Waiting for my love
There may be stardust in the air
Or maybe just some fireflies
You know, I will be here underneath the sky
Waiting to gaze into your eyes

And if it should take the whole evening
And long into the day
Still, I wait to see your face, my dear
As I look up to pray
Return to me, my darling
Life cannot exist without you
I know that far across this sea of sky
You wait for me, too

The moon is hanging low tonight -
The stars are twinkling all about
And I will be here until morning's light
Until my true love - is found

Under the moon
I will be hanging around
Until my true love - is found

Moonglow

Gazing down on me
Observing from a distance
Moonglow
What is it you see?
Watching with insistence
Your bright leads my mood astray
As I wait for break-of-day
My heart is an open page
With your direction, my destiny staged

Moonglow
You enter gently through twilight

Moonglow
Your light piercing through the sky
Ruling the darkness of night
On you, my looming fate relies
Surrounded by your moon glow
Love's truth be told, my heart is sure to know
The mate my soul destined to behold

As life continues to unfold
Underneath your moon glow

Moonglow
Looking down on me
Is it everything you see?
My heart aches for a sign
That there is a true love to be mine
Will I meet him tonight?
Under the stream of beaming light

Moonglow

Doubting Hearts

If people aren't told, how can they truly know?
Doubt begins to grow
Sheltering the heart can come at quite a cost
Passions protected can bring about
Something special lost
Words spoken can seal the heart's fate
Feelings gone unspoken
Cause hearts to break
If people aren't told, how can they truly know?
Doubt begins to grow

Happily Never After

Once upon a time, there was a woman
Who bared her soul to the man in her dreams
She whispered to him often
How she longed for the day they would meet
She kept her heart open and waiting
Hoping mutual feelings, he would speak
But always he left her in silence
To wander a one-sided street

Once upon a time, there was a woman
Awakened by the man in her dreams
When he refused to speak
She opened her eyes to defeat
Silence is only golden while asleep

Marriage Made in Heaven

Once the sizzle simmers down
And sparks no longer fly
That marriage made in heaven
Ultimately dies
When passion's flame refuses to ignite
Empty darkness will ensue
Extinguishing love's light

Left in a haze of feelings – uncertain
Vulnerable hearts stay hidden
Behind their emotional curtains
With promises continuing to fade
For the marriage made in heaven
There is nothing left to save

Forever Wanderer

The forever wanderer sees his love –
Then swiftly darts right past
For with the wanderer
True love can never last
He chooses friends with caution
Keeping none too close for long
When he begins to feel his heartstrings pulled
In a heartbeat, he is gone

The forever wanderer longs to find the right one
But if he ever does, only quicker he will run

If there is a woman who could fulfill his every need
She would only give him motivation to gain speed

For in his frantic search, he fails to recognize
To his truth, he is forever blind
If he continues to stand in fate's way
Indeed, love will never stay

The eyes of a wanderer will always be looking
But his perception
Will never be found
Because every time love makes her presence
His ~ will be gone

Remaining Friend

From the beginning, through the middle, to the end

In the beginning, there was
The attraction
Love at first sight - or just a chemical reaction?
Two lonely beings
One chance meeting

At his - first glance - he was taken by her trance
At her - first glance - he made her laugh
Neither expected
Their hearts would react
That day their souls first met
By chance

Pretty soon
A friendship grew
Neither expected
Love to bloom

Talking and laughing – minutes tick-tock into hours
Both under the spell and strength
Of cupid's arrow's power
Neither expecting the emotional entwine
As lives begin to unwind
From that one chance meeting
In the blink of an eye

The heart of one's soul knows no bounds
And fate does not conform to mortal time
One's life was free
For the other – gold rings bind

In the beginning
There was the newness of romance
Blind by love
They both took a chance
But over time
Realizations came to mind
Now
Somehow
The two must find
A way back to the normalcy
In the lives
They left behind

Neither expecting
Love shared, to end
To preserve the relationship of friend

From the beginning—through the middle—to the end

Forever my love
My friend

Beautiful Soul

In this world – like you
Sadly
There are few
Beautiful soul, do you know how I adore you?
When you see my gaze falling deep into your eyes
Is your heart left with a glimpse of a clue?
Beautiful soul, how I wish I could be near you
Every waking hour of my day
Whispering to you
Words I long to say

Sharing sentiments with your heart
That mine has yearned to convey
But past mistakes are binding
And futures remain undefined
Wanting for something, we struggle with how
Yet, attempt to reconcile ourselves
To the places for which we are bound
Our minds wrestle with questions of – why?
While resigning to what is now

Knowing to not ask of fate
More than what fate is willing to allow
Will my heart's desire be quenched?
And does yours thirst, too?
Will regret, be the aftertaste of our tomorrow
Haunting us both for our failure to follow through?

Before you,
I had been drenched in sorrow
In an existence filled with mundane
Beautiful soul, how you have blessed my world
by immersing it in change
My present
Transformed
Into a happy place
For in it, there is you

Sadly
In this world
Beautiful souls
Are few
I'm glad in mine, there's you

The Choices We Make
– are the Chances We Take

By chance, we met
By choice, we've kept
Our friendship still grows strong
I love you to the moon and back
Forever as the day is long

Love beats our hearts in unison
With each more in sync, we become
The chance of there not being an - us
Would be the choice of neither one

The choices we make are the chances we take
If given the chance all over again
I'd choose to take it with you

Abc-123-Loving You is E-E-Z

I love you from A-Z
And everything in-between
It's so easy as one, two, three
To love you t-o-t-a-l-l-y
You have taught me along the way
To view the world with eyes unafraid
Broaden my horizons with each new day
Avoid what starts and ends with same

Living with intention comes easy for you
And this you've imparted to me
To love from A-Z
Is to love unconditionally
It's so easy as one, two, three
To love you t-o-t-a-l-l-y

Lost Then Found

In his losing me
I found him
Love once free
Now considered sin
Winners never lose
Except when those lost
Win

Without You

I sigh
I cry
In my heart, every day
I die
The unhappiness
I can no longer bear
Living in my world of despair

Perhaps you are listening -
Somewhere
I wonder if you are out there
I wonder if you care
I sigh
I cry
Every day, without your heart
I die
I wait
When I look into your eyes
I see your heart
It is so big
So genuine
So, kind

I wait in suspended time
I wait for your heart to be mine
Can you see mine waiting
While looking in my eyes?

Cupid Take Down That Wall

A tap, tap, tap on the wall
Surrounding and guarding your heart
A crack develops
Soon, more crevasses form
The walls shatter
Exposing the heart, torn
Now on its mend
When love anew is born

Directly Indirect

When it comes to matters of your heart
Your secret remains kept
Not to allow any room, for regret
You faithfully walk the fine line of being
Directly indirect

When it comes to matters of the heart
The secret
Must be kept
Make no room for regret
Do not emotionally invest
Remain on the path
To loneliness
By faithfully walking the fine line of being
Directly indirect

The Best is Yet to Be

The friendship needs to grow some
Before the love can come into full bloom

Sometimes it's just too soon
For matters of the heart
Cannot be rushed into

Let nature take its course
Is what's always best to do
For what will be, will be
For me, for you

Sew the Spider Weaves His Web

You are my Charlotte
You've brought to light an intimate
Once buried in my dark
Re-taught me pieces of integrity
Lost
Yet essential to maintain
A reverence of the heart

Important childhood lessons learned
To build a character, strong
Vulnerable to the world's living form
Where humanity has gone wrong
Disguising our morals as gone

You have been the charlotte
To my soul's awakening to what is right
Sewing bits of knowledge into the tapestry of my life

Like a single prominent thread weaving insight
That without the very fabric of wisdom
To treat nature as - our friend

The ecological pattern necessary for our existence
Will come tragically to an end

You have been my Charlotte
Sew the spider
Weaves his web
Perhaps our humanity will mend

Tapestry

You are part of the tapestry
that weaves love into my life
Thank you

I Found a Heart Today

As I walked along my way

I wonder what there could be

How many heart-shaped objects
Can one person be privileged to see?

In this lifetime of uncertainties

What in the world could this universe
Be trying to tell me
With so many different hearts that I've seen

I found a heart today,
I wonder if it found me
I wonder if it's your heart, I, see?

On the Mend

There will be an un-mendable tear,

But our most comfortable things in life

Usually do, show some wear

My forever wanderer

The cape fits

The following pages contain selections from my other publications and a little about myself.

From my book:
A cup of Inspiration to Go Please –
My Heart Runneth Over

By Invitation Only

The universe has sent out signs
We heed their message
Their truths we won't deny
The fate – it lies within the grasp
Provided it's our time

I Ponder

Since the past does not exist at all
In the minute blip of time in which it occurs
It is gone
Then why do we insist on letting it
In our minds - live on?
Why do we let something
Non-existent
Wreak such havoc in our lives
By allowing it to be a memory
That continues on and on?
Let it go –
The universe did a long time ago

From my book:
Locks of Love – A Book of Encouragement

Poetry has the power to uplift the spirits of those who feel weary and to alleviate the emotional pain that can arise when both the body and mind are suffering. Release the burdens that hold down your spirit, whether you are experiencing physical pain or struggling with emotional and mental challenges. Regardless of the difficulties you may be facing, allow your spirit to find rest in the hope and assurance that your future is always secured in the great mercy, love, and promise of Your Higher Power.

Hopes Bright
Life
Stolen from us when we are feeling submerged in depression,
a deadly current.
Hope
A life jacket God gives us.

When darkness grows thicker around us,
Hope is a distant brightness
Just barely visible to our naked eye.
It appears to be surrounded by and covered with a veil of
darkness.
It glistens but is unreachable from our grasp.
But through the delicately woven fabric of emotions, we can
see its bright persistence to shine through.
As we trudge through our darkness, we frantically reach to
pull away the veil, but the fog of gloom that suffocates us
keeps pushing us back, further away from hope's shining
force.

A will of perseverance that is not our own pulls us through
the debilitating thickness of our night. The veil lifts just
enough to fill our lungs with a resuscitative gasp as if we were
drowning, our lungs now emptied of their liquid death; we are
finally able to breathe in the freshness of a new day.

Faith pushes, while the brightness of hope pulls us through the darkest patches of our journey, and grace gives us nourishment while we trudge through
Life.

A Gentle Rain of Tears

What makes a grown woman cry?
Just about anything
At any given time

Whenever we feel weary, broken, and alone,
To wash away the heartache
Let tears flow
To clear out the crevices where despair gets trapped
In the darkest areas of our souls
Like a gentle rain, our tears cleanse,
Until once again, we feel whole

The Roads We Choose

Rough roads are never the paths we choose for ourselves.
They are simply a reality of the journey of our natural lives.
God allows these detours that lead us to the narrow path,
where he awaits.

From my book:
A Line in the Sand –
A Journey Towards Forgiveness

For those who struggle to forgive and those who long for
forgiveness ~

Tunnel vision

I had to go through the dark tunnel to get to the light
Now that I have,
I think I will survive

We Walk

Our journey takes us down many roads,
And many challenges show their face.
But through the thickest part of the forest, we walk,
Our steps can be lighter with grace.

We will no doubt cross many bridges,
And some we will burn down, too.
But at the end of our darkened tunnel,
We will see a glimmer,
And in that instance, we will know,
We've been guided the whole way by You.

Be the Bulldozer ~ Not the Ground

Until you stop seeing yourself as a victim
You will never get anywhere in life.

You did not have it any worse
Than anybody else growing up.

Or maybe you did, but,

Everyone has fallout in their life.

From which the debris is not always easy to discard.

Emotional wounds leave painful scars.

The secret to success,

Is to leave all of it in the dust.

Move forward,

Plow past,

Be the person in your dream.

Issues that paralyze,

Transform them to be what propel you,

Leap into a new today.

Stop letting the past prey upon your future.

Forgive,

Forget,

Move on.

Be the bulldozer, not the ground.

About the Author

Holly coop resides in the Midwest with her husband,
children, and furry friends.
Holly enjoys writing and publishing inspirational poetry,
motivational quotes, and spiritual insights. She has authored
five poetry collections. Touching hearts with words has
become her life purpose. She hopes her words will stir hearts
and inspire others in their purpose. In addition to writing,
holly enjoys sketching, photography, and creating art
featuring her poetry.
Holly invites readers to visit her at
hollycoopauthor.wordpress.com - where she shares
reflections, nuggets of wisdom, and anything that comes to
mind.

Thank you for all your support.

Poetry is an art form that can change hearts and minds,
open new visions for our society, and change our world,
one word at a time. I'm blessed to be able to share my love
of the written art of poetry with you.
~ Holly

HollyCoopBooks.com

The End